YOUR NEW PENSIONS CHOICE
[Third Edition]

Your New Pensions Choice

An explanatory guide

Third Edition

John V. Wilson FCA

Bryn Davies BSc (Econ), FIA
of Bacon & Woodrow

Tolley Publishing Company Limited
A BENN GROUP PUBLICATION

First edition: July 1987
Second edition: September 1987
Reprinted: January 1988
Third edition: March 1988

Published by
Tolley Publishing Company Ltd
Tolley House
17 Scarbrook Road
Croydon CR0 1SQ England
01-686 9141

Typeset by
C. Leggett & Son Ltd, Mitcham, Surrey

Printed in Great Britain by
Dotesios (Printers) Ltd,
Bradford-on-Avon, Wiltshire

ISBN 0 85459 342-X

Contents

CONTENTS

About this book

We hope this book will prove to be helpful to the millions (literally) of individuals who, by July 1988, will be able to decide for themselves how they wish to make pension provision in the years ahead.

Without doubt, the majority of employees who are fortunate enough already to be, or to be able to become, members of an occupational pension scheme will be better off by remaining members of that scheme. However, there are exceptions to this general rule which we point out in Chapter 9, and all pension scheme members should be aware of the new AVC arrangements described in Chapter 5.

Writing this book has proved to be a little like trying to shoot at a moving target. In the week before publication of the first edition a further twenty sets of regulations under the Social Security Act 1986 were published and the second Finance Act 1987 was passed through parliament. On 26 August, the government announced that the starting date for personal pensions was postponed until 1 July 1988.

We have tried to explain all the new pensions legislation in a way which everyone will be able to understand. In Chapter 9 we give some advice on how to decide what to do and the factors which should be taken into consideration before reaching that decision.

We are most grateful for the help we have received from the DHSS, the Inland Revenue, Alan Maxwell, and our own colleagues. We also want to thank our printers for their continuing patience.

JOHN WILSON
BRYN DAVIES

2 September 1987

1
Introduction

Note on third edition

This third edition has been updated to include changes introduced or proposed by 15 March 1988 (Budget Day).

A pensions revolution is taking place in the UK. By July 1988, important new ways by which you can provide for your retirement will be in operation. These include the new concept of personal pensions, additional facilities to enable you to increase your pension yet remain a member of your employers' pension scheme, and forthcoming changes in the State Earnings Related Pension Scheme.

Everyone has new alternatives to consider, new choices to make – particularly if you are employed.

This short book first explains the new legislation, how and when it is being introduced, and how it will work alongside existing pensions law and practice.

It next sets out clearly the various alternatives which will become available to you. To find out, all you have to do is to decide to which of the five categories of employment listed below you belong.

Finally, it gives you independent, unbiased advice to help you make the right pension choice in your present circumstances and taking into account your likely career pattern in the years ahead.

No previous knowledge of pensions or pensions terms is needed when reading this book. Technical terms, indicated with an asterisk*, are explained in 'boxes' as they first arise in the text, and again in the glossary to be found at the end of the book.

Please note that throughout this book the phrase *pension scheme* **is**

1

only used to mean an *occupational* **pension scheme**, i.e. one run by your employers (or perhaps within your employers' trade or profession) and which you and your fellow employees can join, either now or when you become eligible. **Similarly personal pensions are always referred to as** *personal pension plans*, to distinguish them from occupational pension schemes.

How this book can help you

The structure of this book is as follows:

Chapter 2 explains the pensions background and sets the current scene. It also summarises all the changes which are being introduced by July 1988.

Chapter 3 tells you which of the alternative ways of providing for your pension will actually be available to you. This will depend upon whether you are now

(a)　employed, and a member of a contracted-out pension scheme*, or

(b)　employed, and a member of a contracted-in pension scheme (i.e. one that has not been contracted-out of SERPS*), or

(c)　employed, but not (yet) a member of any pension scheme, or

(d)　self-employed, responsible for your own national insurance contributions and income tax on your earnings, or

(e)　unemployed, for any reason.

---

 * A *contracted-out pension scheme* is one whose members have been contracted-out of the *State Earnings Related Pension Scheme* ('SERPS') (see Chapter 7).

It can only be contracted-out if it is approved by the Inland Revenue and if it satisfies certain conditions laid down by the Occupational Pensions Board (an independent government appointed body). These can now include either the provision

---

> of a *guaranteed minimum pension* ('GMP') to members (approximately equal to that receivable under SERPS) or minimum contributions.

If you are in any doubt as to whether your pension scheme is contracted-out or contracted-in, ask your employer to tell you.

Having found out in Chapter 3 which alternatives are open to you, you can decide which of the next three chapters you need to study carefully.

Chapter 4 deals in detail with personal pension plans, setting out their advantages and disadvantages.

Chapter 5 explains the new rules on AVCs*, setting out their advantages and disadvantages.

> * AVCs are additional voluntary contributions which a member of a pension scheme can make to increase his or her pension at retirement.

Chapter 6 deals with your employers and your present pension scheme. It reminds you to consider carefully the benefits provided by your pension scheme, and the contributions which you and your employers make to it. It also encourages you to find out from your employers how they intend to react to the introduction of personal pension plans and whether they are likely to make any changes to their pension scheme in the foreseeable future.

Two general chapters follow. *Chapter 7* is a reminder about how the present State Pension Schemes work. *Chapter 8* covers a range of subjects such as pensions mortgages*, equal retirement ages, early and late retirement, and the position in situations such as prolonged absences from work or death in service.

> * *Pension mortgages* are loans for house purchase or improvements, repayable from lump sums provided by pension arrangements (see Chapter 8).

Chapter 9 is perhaps the most important in the book. It sets out to give independent, unbiased advice to help you make the most sensible choice taking into account factors such as your age, your length of service with your present employers, the likelihood of your changing jobs in the years ahead, the terms of your employers' present pension scheme(s), how much you have to contribute now to your pension scheme, whether you will be better off in or out of SERPS, etc . . . Some examples of typical employment situations are given, covering cases where the pensions choice is easy to make and others where the choice is marginal and much more difficult.

The *Appendices* which follow comprise

A.   Effect of inflation table.
B.   A summary of a pension scheme members' rights on leaving pensionable service* before retirement.

> * *Leaving pensionable service* means leaving your employer's pension scheme for any reason.

Finally, never make a hasty decision on this important subject before studying carefully all the pros and cons of the alternatives now becoming open to you. The wrong decision now may cost you or your dependants thousands of pounds in lost pensions or life assurance benefits in the years to come.

2
The background: where we are now

This chapter summarises the current pensions scene, and provides the necessary background for the rest of this book.

Why you should provide for your retirement

You need to save or provide for retirement for the obvious reason that you will lose your earnings from your work when you retire. At the same time as putting money aside for your pension, it is normal also to cover other events such as death or long term ill-health so as to provide financial protection for your spouse and other dependants.

How you can provide for your retirement now
(The changes being introduced are explained later in this chapter).

(a)   **For the employee**

The available methods are:

(1)   **The two State schemes** viz

(i)   *The flat rate scheme* which provides a pension of an amount fixed by the government each year, regardless of the level of your pre-retirement earnings. From 11 April 1988, the flat rate pension is £41.15 per week for a single person, £65.90 per week for a married couple where the wife was not a contributor. If both husband and wife were contributors, the combined pension is $2 \times £41.15 = £82.30$ per week.

(ii) *Through the State Earnings Related Pension Scheme*, (SERPS), which provides an additional pension based on your pay between 'band earnings' for national insurance purposes, the band being changed each year (see page 25).

Every employee has to participate in the flat rate scheme by paying national insurance contributions deducted from pay. Your employers also have to pay national insurance contributions on your behalf.

However, you can be contracted-out of SERPS by being a member of a contracted-out pension scheme run by your employers. Both you and they then pay national insurance contributions at the lower contracted-out rate.

There is more about these two State schemes in Chapter 7.

(2) A pension scheme run by your employer

Known more fully as occupational pension schemes, these are now invariably schemes which are approved by the Inland Revenue. For a pension scheme to be approved it must meet certain requirements of the Inland Revenue, including limits on benefits provided under the scheme. Only an approved pension scheme enjoys the following taxation privileges:

(i)   tax relief is given on employee contributions by deduction from income before income tax is calculated

(ii) tax relief is given to employers by allowing their contributions as an expense for tax purposes

(iii) income and capital gains of the pension scheme are tax-free

(iv) tax-free lump sums (within limits) can be paid by the scheme to members on retirement. (But pensions paid are treated as taxable income of the recipient).

Pension schemes can be *contracted-out* of SERPS (as explained in Chapter 1), or *contracted-in*, i.e. not contracted-out.

They will be either *non-contributory** or *contributory**

---

* *Non-contributory* means that only the employer pays contributions towards the scheme, usually as a percentage of pay.

* *Contributory* means that both employer and employee pay contributions, usually as a percentage of pay.

Pension schemes will be *insured* or *self-administered*. An insured scheme is one where the contributions are paid to an insurance company who undertakes in return to pay some or all the benefits provided under the scheme. Most large pension schemes are now self-administered where the contributions are paid to the trustees of the scheme for direct investment, under the advice of specialist in-house or external investment managers.

Pension schemes will also be either *defined benefit** schemes or *defined contribution** schemes.

---

* A *defined benefit* scheme is one under which the pension benefits are fixed at your retirement regardless of the investment performance of the scheme. The benefits are usually calculated as 1/60th or 1/80th of your pensionable pay (see below) immediately prior to your retirement, for each year of 'pensionable service' (employment by your employer which counts towards your pension entitlement). This is why defined benefit schemes are usually known as *'final salary'* schemes.

Any contribution by you as an employee is normally a fixed percentage of your *pensionable pay* (the pay on which your pension will be based, which in some schemes may be your normal pay less an amount such as the lower earnings level for national insurance), but your employers undertake to put into the scheme **whatever is necessary** to provide the scheme's members with the defined benefits.

* A *defined contribution* scheme is in contrast one in which the contributions for either or both employers and employee are at agreed rates, the ultimate benefits being dependent on the value of the fund built up by contributions paid and income

---

> from its investments during your membership of the scheme.
> The fund is used to purchase you a pension on your retirement.
> These schemes are usually known as *'money purchase'* schemes.

You can add to your pension benefits from a pension scheme by making additional voluntary contributions (AVCs) to that scheme provided

(i)   the scheme offers AVC facilities

(ii) your AVCs plus your ordinary contributions as a scheme member (if any) do not exceed 15% of your salary

(iii) the benefits arising from your AVCs plus those from the pension scheme do not exceed Inland Revenue limits.

AVCs are explained fully in Chapter 5.

(3)   **Retirement annuities** (known as 'S.226 policies').

If you are an employee, you can only contribute towards one of these policies if you are not a member of a pension scheme. The maximum you can contribute is 17½% of your earnings (or higher if you were born before 1934). Contributions have to be made to an insurance policy and will then accumulate free of income tax and capital gains tax to provide a lump sum from which an annuity must be purchased on your retirement. The policy can also provide limited death benefits, and a tax-free lump sum on retirement which must not exceed three times the remaining pension.

(4)   **Private savings**

Private savings through regular contributions to a building society, unit trust under a personal equity plan, etc. However, these forms of saving have to be made out of taxed income and do not enjoy the same privileged tax treatment as an approved pension scheme or retirement annuity (see above).

(b)   **For the self-employed**

The available methods are:

(1) **The State flat rate scheme** (see above) towards which you have to pay Class 2 national insurance contributions. You cannot participate in SERPS as a self-employed person.

(2) **Retirement annuities** (known as S.226 policies)
As for an employee (see (3) above).

(3) **Private savings**
As for an employee (see (4) above).

The changes which are coming

(a) **Personal pensions**

These are a new form of tax-efficient pension plan, introduced by the government under the Social Security Act 1986 and the Finance Act (No 2) 1987.

Personal pension plans can be taken out from 1 July 1988 by employees who are not members of a pension scheme, and by anyone self-employed.

If you are an employee and one of your personal pension plans is an *appropriate** one, you can use it to contract-out of SERPS.

> * An *appropriate personal pension plan* is one which, by satisfying certain conditions under the Social Security Act 1986 and by being approved by the Occupational Pensions Board, enables the contributor to the plan to be contracted-out of SERPS (see Chapter 4).

Personal pensions are explained fully in Chapter 4.

(b) **Changes in SERPS**

The pension benefits receivable under SERPS will be reduced for those retiring from the year 2000 onwards.

A 2% incentive is being offered by the DHSS (Department of Health and Social Security) for up to six years to 6 April 1993 to those who contract-out before that date.

You will find further information on SERPS in Chapter 7, and whether or not you should now consider contracting-out in Chapter 9.

(c) Additional voluntary contributions

(i) From 8 April 1987, new AVCs cannot be used to provide additional tax-free lump sums on retirement, but amounts contributed to AVC can be varied more than before.

(ii) From 26 October 1987, you can take out 'free-standing' AVCs*.

> * *Free-standing AVCs* are contributions to an insurance policy or building society outside your pension scheme, which can be used to increase your pension benefits (subject to Inland Revenue limits).

(iii) From 6 April 1988, all pension schemes must offer 'in-scheme' AVC* facilities.

> * *In-scheme AVCs* are those paid to an insurance policy or building society chosen by your pension scheme, or to the scheme itself.

(iv) If you are a member of a contracted-in pension scheme, you can use one AVC policy to contract-out of SERPS so long as it meets the conditions for an appropriate personal pension.

AVCs are explained in more detail in Chapter 5.

(d) On pension schemes generally

(i) From 6 April 1988, it will be possible for a pension scheme to contract-out on the basis of a guaranteed rate of contribution from the employer (and possibly the employee) as an alternative to the present method of contracting-out by promising to pay

GMPs. Such schemes are known as 'COMPS' – contracted-out money purchase schemes.

(ii)   If you are a member of a pension scheme but leave your employers' service early, i.e. before reaching retirement age, the value of your accrued benefits is now more protected against inflation in the future. Also from 6 April 1988, you will be entitled to the benefits accrued after two or more years service instead of five (see Chapter 6 and Appendix B).

(iii) Membership of a pension scheme cannot continue to be compulsory on or after 6 April 1988, unless that scheme is non-contributory and provides only death benefits.

(iv)   There are new requirements for further disclosure of information about a pension scheme to its members. The format of pension scheme accounts is also being changed.

(v)   Excess surpluses on final salary pension schemes will be taxed in future unless the surpluses are used to improve benefits or reduce contributions.

(vi)   Recent financial services legislation places new responsibilities on employers and on trustees of pension schemes.

(vii) The 'Big Bang' in the City in October 1986 has made investment of pension scheme funds less costly, but in a climate which is now both more competitive and more international than before. New techniques for maximising investment returns are becoming available such as programme trading, index funds and the use of futures and options.

You will see from this background summary that a large number of changes are taking place by July 1988. The rest of this guide explains some of these changes more fully, and ends with a chapter giving advice on how best to choose between all the alternatives now becoming available to you.

3
The choices available

The alternatives available to you under the new legislation, and the dates from which you can enter into any new arrangements, depend upon whether you are now or are likely to be:

(A) Employed and a member of a pension scheme which is contracted-out of SERPS, or

(B) Employed and a member of a pension scheme which is not contracted-out of SERPS, or

(C) Employed but not a member of a pension scheme, either because:

- the employer has no pension scheme, or

- membership of the pension scheme is voluntary (and you have declined to join), or

- your age or length of service or terms of employment (e.g. you work only part-time) preclude you from being eligible to join, at least for the time being.

You are also in this category if you are a member of a scheme run by your employer which provides **only** death in service benefits and/or widow's or other dependant's benefits.

(D) Self-employed, or

(E) Unemployed.

The choices available under each of these categories are explained on the following pages.

Advice to help you make the best choice in your present and likely future circumstances is given in Chapter 9.

3 — THE CHOICES AVAILABLE

(A) Employed and member of a contracted-out pension scheme

You can do one of the following:

- Remain a member and **take no further action**.

- Remain a member but increase your pension benefits by making or increasing **additional voluntary contributions (AVCs)** *within your pension scheme*. From April 1987, if your pension scheme rules permit, you have been free to vary the amount and timings of AVC payments as you wish, provided you adhere to the Inland Revenue limitations, explained in Chapter 5. Note also that if your pension scheme has no AVC facilities yet, under the Social Security Act 1986 it must change its rules to permit members to make AVCs from 6 April 1988 onwards.

- Remain a member but increase your pension benefits by making **'free-standing' AVCs outside your pension scheme**. This facility only came into operation from 26 October 1987 onwards.

- Opt out of membership of your pension scheme

  (a) in favour of a **S.226 policy** (but only until 30 June 1988) or

  (b) in favour of a **personal pension plan** (but only on or after 1 July 1988). You will be entitled to a 2% incentive payment from the DHSS up to 5 April 1993 if your personal pension plan is an appropriate one (see Chapter 4), and you have not been in your present contracted-out employment for more than 2 years (see page 25) or

  (c) and make **no provision** for pension other than through the State schemes.

  Unless membership of your pension scheme is voluntary, however, you can only opt out on or after 6 April 1988, the date from which membership of all pension schemes ceases to be compulsory.

Personal pension plans are explained fully in Chapter 4, and the State schemes in Chapter 7.

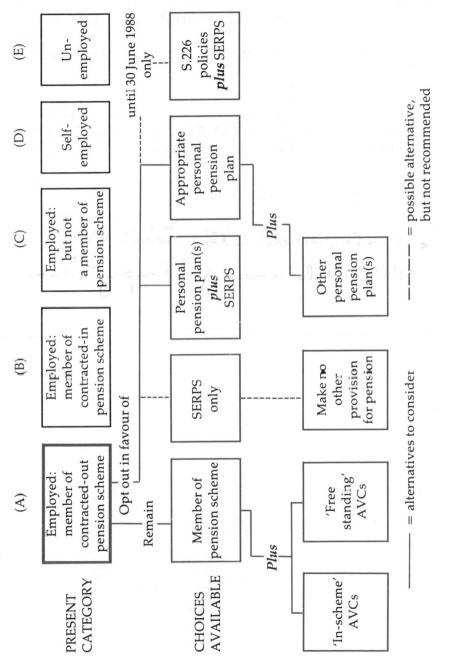

PRESENT CATEGORY

(A) Employed: member of contracted-out pension scheme

(B) Employed: member of contracted-in pension scheme

(C) Employed: but not a member of pension scheme

(D) Self-employed

(E) Un-employed

until 30 June 1988 only

Remain

Opt out in favour of

CHOICES AVAILABLE

Member of pension scheme

Plus

'In-scheme' AVCs

'Free standing' AVCs

SERPS only

Make no other provision for pension

Personal pension plan(s) plus SERPS

Plus

Other personal pension plan(s)

Appropriate personal pension plan

S.226 policies plus SERPS

——— = alternatives to consider

- - - - - = possible alternative, but not recommended

15

(B) Employed and member of a contracted-in pension scheme

You have exactly the same choices as in (A) above with two important additions.

- If you opt out in favour of an appropriate personal pension plan, you will be entitled to a 2% incentive payment from the DHSS for up to six years to 5 April 1993. Personal pension plans and this incentive are explained fully in Chapter 4.

- You may be able to contract-out of SERPS through a 'free-standing' AVC (see page 40).

- Can Contract out with a Rebate Only P.P.P. while remaining in Company Scheme.

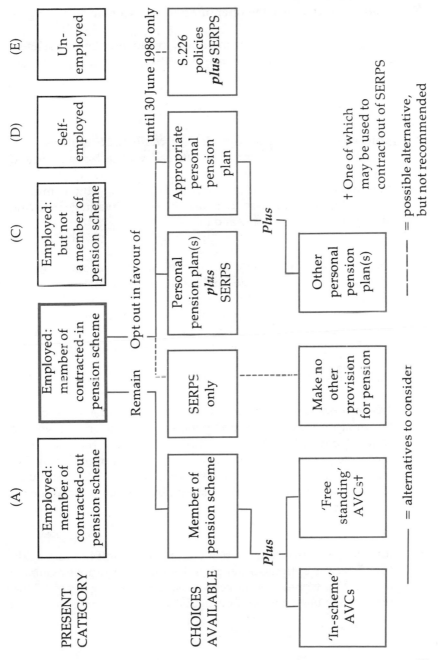

(C) Employed, but not a member of a pension scheme

(Note: This category includes members of an employers' scheme which provides **only** death in service benefits and/or widow's or other dependant's benefits.)

Until 30 June 1988, you can either

- Continue with or take out one or more **S.226 policies** (see Chapter 2, page 8) to provide yourself with a lump sum and pension on retirement. Lump sum benefits allowed on retirement can be greater under a S.226 policy than under a personal pension plan, so there may be some advantage in taking out such a policy before that date,

    or

- Join the **pension scheme** when and if you become eligible. Thereafter you will have the same future choices as either Category (A) or (B) above, depending upon whether your employers' pension scheme is (A) contracted-out or (B) not contracted-out. You would then have to cease contributing to your S.226 policies which would be treated as paid-up.

On or after 1 July 1988, you can either

- Take out one or more **personal pension plans**, one of which can be an appropriate personal pension plan to enable you to contract out of SERPS and possibly also enjoy the 2% DHSS incentive payment. This does not prevent you from continuing with any existing S.226 policies provided your total premiums still remain within the limits allowed by the Inland Revenue for personal pensions,

    or

- Join the **pension scheme** when you become eligible – and again then have the options under categories (A) or (B) above available to you. You would then have to cease contributing to your S.226 policies (or personal pension plans) which would be treated as paid-up,

    or

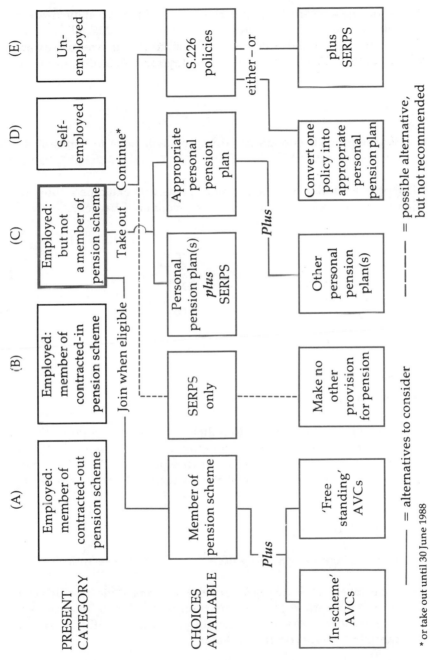

	(A)	(B)	(C)	(D)	(E)
PRESENT CATEGORY	Employed: member of contracted-out pension scheme	Employed: member of contracted-in pension scheme	Employed: but not a member of pension scheme	Self-employed	Un-employed

CHOICES AVAILABLE

- Member of pension scheme
  - *Plus*
    - 'In-scheme' AVCs
    - 'Free standing' AVCs

- Join when eligible
- SERPS only
  - Make no other provision for pension

- Take out / Continue*
- Personal pension plan(s) *plus* SERPS
- Appropriate personal pension plan
  - *Plus*
    - Other personal pension plan(s)
    - Convert one policy into appropriate personal pension plan

- S.226 policies
  - either – or
    - plus SERPS

―――― = alternatives to consider

― ― ― ― = possible alternative, but not recommended

* or take out until 30 June 1988

19

- Continue with any **S.226 policies** you already have. If the insurer allows, you may be able to convert one of these S.226 policies into an appropriate personal pension plan, to enable you to contract out of SERPS and possibly also enjoy the 2% DHSS incentive payment,

  or

- **Do nothing.** If you do nothing, you will have to continue to contribute to SERPS.

S.226 policies and personal pension plans are explained fully in Chapters 2 and 4 respectively. SERPS is covered in Chapter 7.

(D) Self-employed

Until 30 June 1988, you can

- Take out one or more **S.226 policies** to provide yourself with a lump sum and a pension at retirement. Lump sum benefits allowed on retirement can be greater under a S.226 policy than under the personal pension plans which replace them after 30 June.

On or after 1 July 1988, you can

- Continue with any **S.226 policies** you already have and/or

- Take out one or more **personal pension plans**, none of which can be an appropriate personal pension plan. This is because as a self-employed person, you cannot participate in SERPS, so you cannot therefore contract-out of it.

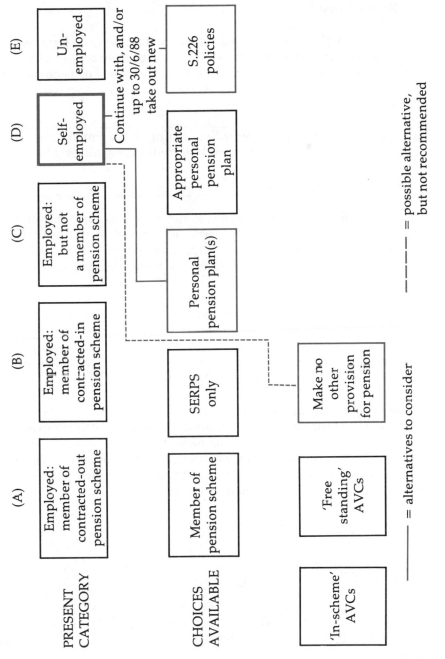

PRESENT CATEGORY

(A) Employed: member of contracted-out pension scheme

(B) Employed: member of contracted-in pension scheme

(C) Employed: but not a member of pension scheme

(D) Self-employed

(E) Un-employed

CHOICES AVAILABLE

Member of pension scheme

SERPS only

Personal pension plan(s)

Appropriate personal pension plan

S.226 policies

Continue with, and/or up to 30/6/88 take out new

'Free standing' AVCs

Make no other provision for pension

'In-scheme' AVCs

———— = alternatives to consider

– – – – = possible alternative, but not recommended

(E) **Unemployed**

If you are unemployed for any reason (e.g. unable to find a job since leaving school, or through redundancy, or because you choose to rely solely on private means), you cannot take out a personal pension plan (or before 1 July 1988 a S.226 policy) because you have no 'net relevant earnings'*.

> * *Net relevant earnings* are, broadly, earnings from employment or as a self-employed person less deductions (other than personal allowances) which can be made to determine your net income for tax purposes.

If you were previously in employment, and were also a member of a pension scheme or schemes, you will be entitled to the benefits secured to date from your and your employers' contributions to those schemes when you retire. Your rights in these circumstances are summarised in Appendix B.

Similarly if you were previously in employment or were previously self-employed, you can treat as paid-up any personal pension plans or S.226 policies you were then contributing to, until such time as you have 'net relevant earnings' again or until you retire (must be after age 50 on personal pension plan, 60 on S.226 policies).

You also cannot participate in SERPS if you are unemployed. It is also possible to continue to pay national insurance contributions voluntarily to ensure your entitlement to certain benefits will continue. **The position is extremely complex and you are strongly recommended to consult your local DHSS office for their help and advice when you are in this situation**.

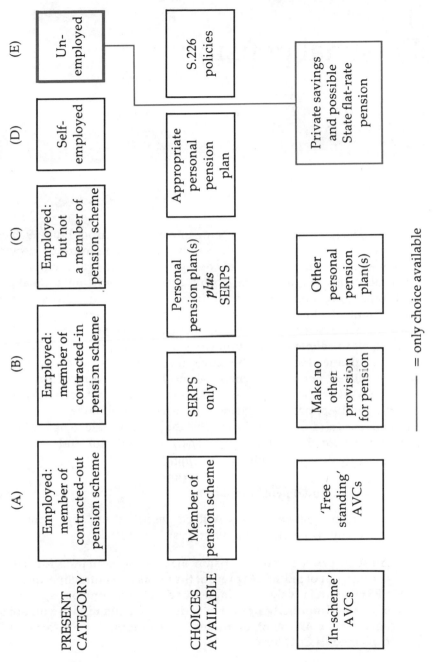

4
Personal pensions

Introduction

Personal pension plans will now come into operation from 1 July 1988. Previously available as S.226 policies, they have been introduced by the government principally to encourage those who are in employment but who are not members of a pension scheme to make additional provision for their retirement, and if they wish, to contract-out of SERPS by making their personal pension plan an *appropriate* one (see below). It is not intended, however, that they will be available to people who continue to be members of their employer's pension scheme. However the government has also decided that membership of pension schemes can no longer be compulsory for employees on or after 6 April 1988. This means that between 6 April and 30 June 1988, pension scheme members can opt out in favour of S.226 policies, and that from 1 July 1988 they will be able to opt out in favour of personal pension plans. The arguments for and against opting out are discussed fully in Chapter 9.

Appropriate personal pension plans

Certain personal pension plans will be described as 'appropriate'. They will enjoy two particular advantages:

(1)   An appropriate personal pension enables you as an individual to contract out of SERPS. At present the terms for contracting-out of SERPS are relatively favourable but do depend on your age and sex. **It will normally be worth serious consideration if you are aged under 49 (men) or under 43 (women)**, for the reasons explained in Chapter 9.

If you take out an appropriate personal pension plan, you and your employers will pay the full, normal rate of national insurance contributions each week or month. However the DHSS will then pay direct to your personal pension plan (see below) a sum equal to the contracting-out rebate, which is the difference between the full and contracted-out rate of national insurance contributions. In addition they will pay a sum equal to the income tax relief due to you on your share of those contributions to your personal pension plan plus the incentive addition (see (2) below).

This is not as complex as it sounds. You may more readily understand how the DHSS contributes towards your appropriate personal pension plan if you look at the example given on page 29 below.

(2) As an encouragement to contract out of SERPS, the DHSS will also make an additional incentive payment to your appropriate personal pension plan until 5 April 1993 *unless* you have been in your present contracted-out job for the two years or more immediately before you start your plan. (In other words you will not be able to obtain this incentive payment if you have been a member of a contracted-out pension scheme, or would have been a member of such a scheme had you been eligible to join but chose not to, for the past two years or more).

The amount of this DHSS incentive is 2% of your 'band earnings'* or £1 per week if greater.

> *Band earnings* is pay falling between the lower and upper earnings limits for national insurance purposes (£39 and £295 per week respectively between 6 April 1987 and 5 April 1988, and £41 and £305 per week from 6 April 1988).

If you start an appropriate personal pension plan on or before 5 April 1989, you can back-date its start to 6 April 1987 (but only for the period you were not a member of a contracted-out scheme) and thus receive the DHSS incentive for up to six years to 5 April 1993.

Appropriate personal pension plans have to satisfy certain conditions under the Social Security Act 1986 and be approved by the Occupational Pensions Board.

Married women (and widows) paying national insurance contributions at the reduced rate cannot take out an appropriate personal pension plan. If you are self-employed you also cannot take out an appropriate personal pension plan. This is because you have not been contributing to SERPS which is only open to employees, and so you cannot contract out of it. But if you subsequently become an employee, you will then be able to convert your personal pension plan to an appropriate one.

The payment of appropriate personal pension plan contributions is dealt with later (page 28). First, some other general points, applicable to all personal pension plans.

Who can take out a personal pension plan and when

If you are aged under 75 you can contribute towards one or more personal pension plans at any one time. You are not, however, allowed to contribute if, at the same time, you are a member of a pension scheme, unless that pension scheme provides only

(a) lump sum benefits on death in service, or

(b) widow's or other dependants' benefits.

Only one plan can be an appropriate one, and the total contributions payable on all the plans must be within the limits explained below.

You cannot start out a personal pension plan before 1 July 1988 under any circumstances, although sometimes it can then be back-dated up to 6 April 1987, as explained in the previous section. If you are a member of a pension scheme but wish to opt out of that scheme and contribute towards a personal pension plan instead, you can only make that switch on or after 1 July 1988.

Whether or not it may be sensible for you to opt out of your pension scheme in favour of a personal pension plan is discussed in Chapter 9.

Portability

Your personal pension plan is fully portable. It belongs to you, and you can take it with you from job to job **without loss**.

Contribution limits

The contributions you pay each year to personal pension plans are fully deductible from your earnings for income tax purposes, but they must be within these limits set by the Inland Revenue:

	% of earnings
If you are age 50 or less†	17.5
51 – 55	20
56 – 60	22.5
61 – 74	27.5

† at the beginning of the tax year (6 April)

Those limits do **not** include the contributions by the DHSS to appropriate personal pension plans but do include any contributions to existing S.226 policies.

If your own contributions are less than these limits, your employers may make contributions up to the balance (they are under no obligation to do so, of course), which would be deductible for tax purposes as an expense of their business. Their contributions are not treated as your income for income tax purposes.

Any unused tax relief for the previous six years can also be claimed. Contributions paid use up first the available relief for the current tax year, the excess then being set off against any unused relief for the previous six years (taking relief in the earliest year first).

Benefits limits

At your retirement the fund built up through all the contributions to your personal pension plan over the years (plus reinvested income and capital growth) must be applied as follows:

(a)   Up to 25% can be paid to you as a tax-free cash lump sum on retirement, subject to an overriding maximum limit for *each* contract, currently £150,000.

However, none of the fund created by the DHSS minimum contributions to an appropriate personal pension plan can be taken as a lump sum. All of that fund must be used to purchase an annuity (see next paragraph).

(b)   The remainder of the fund must be used to purchase an annuity (i.e. pension for life) from an approved insurance company, on retirement between the ages of 50 and 75. Special rules apply to the annuity benefits secured by the DHSS minimum contributions. These must be used to provide an annuity from age 65 or later for men and age 60 or later for women, calculated on 'unisex' rates (i.e. the same rates for men and women of the same age). Furthermore the annuity must increase annually by 3% or the rise in the Retail Prices Index (whichever is the less), and in most cases, after the person receiving the original annuity dies, provide a 50% pension for the life of the widow or widower.

Payment of contributions to an appropriate personal pension plan

The way in which contributions to an appropriate personal pension plan reach the plan (see below) is complicated.

First, *you* will only pay direct to the personal pension provider the premium you have elected to pay *less* income tax at the current basic rate (25% for the tax year 6 April 1988 to 5 April 1989). This is because the Inland Revenue will be operating a scheme for **all** personal pension plans **taken out by employees** similar to the one they now use to give mortgage interest tax relief at source (the 'MIRAS' scheme). Contributions to personal pension plans by individuals **who are self-employed** have to be paid gross.

Employers are unlikely to agree to deduct your personal pension plan contributions from pay, so you will probably need to enter into a standing order on your own bank account.

As previously explained you and your employer will still have to pay the full rate of national insurance contributions each week or month when you are paid your net wage or salary.

Secondly, the *Inland Revenue* will pay the basic income tax deducted from your premium over to your personal pension plan direct, but possibly not until after the end of each tax year (5 April).

Thirdly, the *DHSS* will pay to your personal pension plan direct after the end of each tax year after employers have sent in their annual returns:

(a)   the difference between the full national insurance contributions you and your employer have paid (see above) and the contracted-out, lower rates of national insurance. This difference, known as the contracted-out rebate, is 5.8% of 'band earnings' for the tax years 1988/89 to 1992/93.

plus

(b)   tax relief at the basic rate of income tax due to you on your proportion of the rebate in (a) above

plus (if payable)

(c)   the DHSS incentive (normally 2% of band earnings) referred to earlier.

Here is an example to show how the payment of contributions will work in practice:

Example 4.1

Assume Mr X, earning £200 per week, decides to contribute £10 per week to an **appropriate** personal pension plan, starting in July 1988. Assume also that the basic rate of income tax in 1988/89 is 25%, the national insurance band earnings are as stated on page 25, and that Mr X is entitled to the 2% DHSS incentive.

	£	£

Mr X will pay each week to the personal pension provider £10 less basic rate income tax @ 25%, deducted at source =   7.50

The *Inland Revenue* will pay, in due course, that tax deducted to the personal pension plan   2.50

The *DHSS* will pay, in due course to the plan:

(a) Both the employers' and the employees' national insurance rebate (3.8% + 2% = 5.8%) on Mr X's band earnings (which are £200 − £41 = £159) =   9.22

(b) Income tax relief due on the employees' national insurance rebate (2%) of Mr X's band earnings @ 25% = 25/75 × 2% of £159 =   1.06

(c) The 2% DHSS incentive on Mr X's band earnings = 2% of £159 =   3.18

                                                              —— 13.46

Giving a total payment to the personal pension plan provider of   £   23.46

Notes (a) The £13.46 represents 8.466% of Mr X's band-earnings (5.8% + ($^{25}/_{75}$ × 2%) + 2%).

(b) In this example the £23.46 works out at 11.73% of Mr X's pay, of which he contributes only 3.75%. But he will lose future SERPS benefit in respect of this employment.

(c) The maximum amount which the DHSS will contribute to an appropriate personal pension plan in 1988/89 will be £1,162 p.a. (8.466% of £264 × 52 weeks). For 1987/88 the maximum DHSS contribution is £1,204 (9.045% of £256 × 52 weeks).

Payment of other personal pension plan contributions

These will follow exactly the same pattern as explained above for appropriate personal pension plans except that there will be no payments from the DHSS. Thus if the assumption given in the above example were unchanged other than that Mr X decided to invest only in an ordinary personal pension plan, he would still pay £7.50 per week and the Inland Revenue £2.50, to give the total premium of £10.

For all types of personal pension plans, **any contributions paid by the employer** will go direct to the plan, gross, with no deduction at source.

Providers of personal pensions

Only the following are allowed to offer personal pension plans

Investment type organisations:	Life assurance companies
	Unit trusts
	Friendly societies
Deposit type organisations:	Banks
	Building Societies

You can switch from one appropriate personal pension provider to another at any time but it is only effective from the beginning or end of each tax year.

Competition is likely to be intense. The regulations under which the selling of each will be controlled are as follows:

Type of Organisation	Appropriate Personal Pensions Plans	Ordinary Personal Pensions Plans
Investment	Securities and Investment Board rules (under Financial Services Act)	Securities and Investment Board rules (under Financial Services Act)
Deposit	DHSS regulations	Bank or Building Society regulations

Administration charges for personal pension plans will not be subject to any specified limit, as the government expect that 'charges will stabilise at acceptable levels as a result of competition and disclosure'. The charges being made have to be disclosed by the plan provider.

From 1 July 1988, quotations for personal pension plans by investment type organisations will have to be given in accordance with two bases laid down by LAUTRO (The Life Assurance and Unit Trust Regulatory Organisation, an organisation approved by the Securities Industry Board).

There are a number of safeguards being created to ensure that personal pension plans are properly and securely managed. There is always an element of risk, though, in any investment and if you decide to begin a personal pension plan you should take particular care in choosing the provider.

How to choose a personal pension plan provider

If you decide you want to invest in a personal pension plan you next have to choose which provider (e.g. insurance company, unit trust, bank, building society or friendly society) you will trust with your money. You also have to decide what kind of personal pension plan you want.

There will be three main kinds of personal pension plans available, though not every provider will sell them all:

(a) *Unit-linked:* Under a unit-linked plan the contributions, after a deduction for commission and expenses, is invested in a unit trust. The amount paid on retirement will depend on how those units fare and can go up or down in line with stock markets. There are no guarantees of any kind on the amount paid at retirement. This type of plan will mainly be provided by unit trusts and life insurance companies.

(b) *With-profits:* The pension at retirement is made up of a basic guaranteed pension plus bonuses. Bonuses will be added each year and will depend on the investment profits of the provider. Future bonuses are not guaranteed.

This type of plan will mainly be provided by life insurance companies.

(c) *Deposit Schemes:* The amount paid on retirement is equal to the original contributions plus interest at a rate which will be fixed from time-to-time in line with rates paid for money held on deposit. These rates are likely, in the longer term, to be unattractive when compared to those available on market investments but are more certain.

This type of plan will mainly be provided by banks and building societies.

To replace the guaranteed benefits from the state scheme in respect of minimum contributions most people will want the level of assurance given by a with-profits plan. For extra contributions some people will be attracted by the possible extra return offered by a unit-linked plan.

There will be many providers offering a wide range of personal pension plans, but they will not all be the same. First their investment returns will vary widely. Secondly they will have different levels of expenses which will be deducted from the contributions you make or the benefits you receive. Thirdly they will have different conditions attaching to the plans.

An important point to remember is that you cannot judge a plan by the projections given to you of what benefits will be provided. These are only estimates and from 1 July 1988 will have to be made on a standard basis (see above). What you can look at is the return which has been achieved in the past and some providers have been able to achieve consistently above-average results. But remember, past results are still no guarantee of what will happen in the future.

You must also remember that a large part of the expenses of most plans is taken up by the commission paid to the agent who sells you the plan. Some providers do not pay commission which suggests that they may be better value, even if they are not recommended by an agent who relies on his or her income from commission.

When anyone tries to sell you a personal pension plan there are a number of questions you should ask before signing anything. And even after you have signed a proposal you will have a 'cooling off' period of 14 days during which you can change your mind without penalty.

The questions to ask of anyone selling you a personal pension plan are:

- Are you tied to selling the products of only one provider or are you advising that this is the best personal pension for me out of all those available?

- How much commission will be paid to you and/or your employer if I take out this personal pension plan?

- What other charges will be deducted from my contributions?

- What will be the amount of money in my personal pension plan after one, two and five years, assuming I continue to contribute at present levels, compared to the contributions I will have paid?

- How much will my pension be at my normal retirement age expressed as a percentage of my forecast final salary at retirement?

- What happens if I retire early for any reason?

- What happens to my personal pension plan if I die before retiring, or when I die after retirement?

- How does your investment performance record over the past five and ten years compare with the projections included in your proposal to me?

- What happens if I cease contributing to my plan with you within one, two, five or ten years?

Transfers of previously accrued benefits to and from personal pension plans

Pension rights which have been accrued in a pension scheme can be transferred to a personal pension plan, subject to certain safeguards. But if you opt out of your present pension scheme without leaving your present employment, you do not have the right to a transfer value of benefits accrued before 6 April 1988 unless your present pension scheme rules allows it.

It will also normally be possible to transfer accrued rights from personal pension plans back to pension schemes provided the scheme agrees.

It is the government's intention that there should be maximum flexibility in the transfer of accrued rights between all forms of pension provision, provided this privilege is not being abused to secure artificial tax advantages.

Advantages of personal pension plans compared with 'final salary' pension schemes

- Portability – no loss on change of job.

- Visible fund, growing year by year.

- There is no limit on pension benefits, only on contributions to the personal pension plan. So full advantage can be gained from particularly favourable investment conditions.

- Your personal pension plan fund benefits if, as in the past ten years, investment annual returns (dividends + capital growth) have been high.

- † Freedom to choose your plan provider and to change at the end of each tax year.

35

- If your salary prior to retirement falls below earlier levels, your pension benefits are protected to some extent.

- Can provide attractive pension benefit for younger staff.

●† May enable you to contract out of SERPS if you wish and thus also enjoy the DHSS incentive for up to six years to 5 April 1993.

- Lump sum cash option on retirement *may* be greater than that available from your pension scheme + AVCs.

Disadvantages of personal pension plans v. 'final salary' pension schemes

- No sort of guarantee by your employer about the level of your retirement benefits.

- Your pension will be less certain because it will not be related to your final salary.

- Your pension at retirement will depend on two other uncertain factors

   (a)   how well your money has been invested, *up to that date*

   (b)   annuity rates *at that date*.

●† Death in service and ill-health benefits will probably be an extra cost to you, if you leave your present pension scheme.

●† Total premiums being paid in are likely to be less than under a pension scheme, as most employers will not wish to contribute towards them. Except for the very young (or the lucky) this in turn will normally mean that less benefit emerges.

- The limitations on contributions which can be made to personal pension plans.

●† You may not be allowed to rejoin your present employer's pension scheme if you subsequently want to – anyway probably not on favourable terms.

●† Any commission to an agent selling you a personal pension plan will be deducted from your contributions to the plan.

●† Administrative charges will be made by the personal pension plan provider and these can sometimes be a significant proportion of the contributions paid. In pension schemes, similar charges are usually borne in full by the employer, and are likely to be lower *pro rata*.

●† Personal pension plans are likely to be poor value if contributions are only made for a short period, due to administrative charges and commission.

● Delay in the receipt of premiums from the Inland Revenue and DHSS (who have to rely on employers' annual returns).

† = applicable also to 'money purchase' pension schemes, as compared with personal pension plans.

5
Additional Voluntary Contributions (AVCs)

Current position

Many pension schemes already allow employee members to make AVCs within the scheme (called *'in-scheme' AVCs*) usually either to an insurance company or to a building society or to one selected by the employee from two or more of such providers offered by the employers' scheme. Some pension schemes allow AVCs direct into the funds of the pension scheme possibly to purchase additional years' service.

Until April 1987 once payments to an in-scheme AVC arrangement had started, they had to continue at the same rate for at least five years. That rule has now been relaxed as explained below.

There were, and are still, two other Inland Revenue limitations on AVCs

(a)   the employee cannot contribute more than 15% of his or her earnings to AVCs and the pension scheme in total and

(b)   the total benefits provided by the AVCs and the pension scheme taken together must not exceed the benefit limits prescribed by the Inland Revenue.

AVCs within these limits are fully allowed as deductions from your income for income tax purposes.

5 — ADDITIONAL VOLUNTARY CONTRIBUTIONS (AVCs)

AVC facilities to become compulsory

All pension schemes will have to offer 'in-scheme' AVC facilities to their members from April 1988 onwards and which in turn will have to offer reasonable value for money. But if your employer has more than one pension scheme, only one of those schemes has to offer 'in-scheme' AVC facilities.

Other changes coming into force

There are two important new concessions on AVCs:

(a) From April 1987, **providing your pension scheme rules permit**, you have been able to vary the amount and timing of AVC contributions as much as you like, subject still to the above Inland Revenue limits. Your employer can refuse to accept 'in-scheme' AVCs below ½% of your taxable earnings *or* three times the National Insurance lower earnings limit (currently £41 per week) in any tax year whichever is the higher.

(b) From 26 October 1987, if you are a member of a pension scheme you have been able to make AVC contributions outside your pension scheme to a plan of your own choice (again subject to the Inland Revenue limits). Life assurance companies and building societies offer such arrangements. These are called 'free-standing' AVCs. Contributions to 'free-standing' AVCs are paid net of basic rate income tax.

Ban on using new AVCs to get larger tax-free lump sums on retirement

There is a major snag, however, to the relaxations described in the preceding paragraph. **Sums paid to new AVCs** (whether 'in-scheme' or 'free-standing') **taken out after 7 April 1987 may only be used to enhance pension benefits and provide life assurance cover**, as they cannot be used to increase the tax-free lump sum available on retirement. Any increases to AVC arrangements in existence prior to 8 April 1987 can be used as before to improve lump sum benefits on retirement (subject to the usual Inland Revenue limits). This rule for new AVCs does not apply to pension schemes where the AVCs, like the pension scheme, provide pension benefits and lump sums in fixed proportions.

AVCs can be contracted-out

If you are a member of a contracted-in pension scheme you will be able to use **one** of your free-standing AVCs to contract-out of SERPS, if it meets the requirements of an appropriate personal pension plan approved by the OPB (see Chapter 4). All the advantages of an appropriate personal pension plan will then be obtainable on that AVC, except that there will be no tax relief on the employee's national insurance rebate.

Advantages of AVCs

- It can be a very tax-efficient way of enhancing your pension, particularly when you can afford to save more from higher earnings.
- From 6 April 1987, you can choose how much you pay and when (subject to the legal minimum if set by your employer – see above).
- From 26 October 1987, you will have much greater freedom to decide to whom you pay your AVC.
- Your employer will deduct 'in-scheme' AVCs from your pay.

Disadvantages of AVCs

- Money saved via AVCs can never be withdrawn prior to retirement.
- New AVCs after 7 April 1987 cannot be used to enhance lump sums on retirement.
- The limitation on contributions.
- Uncertainty about your actual pension benefits secured by AVCs.
- If your total benefits from your pension scheme and AVCs exceed Inland Revenue limits, the scheme benefits will have to be cut back.

6
Your employer

The importance of finding out about your employers' attitude towards the new pension regime coming into force by 1 July 1988 has been stressed already in Chapter 1.

This chapter summarises first the changes which your employers will have to make to their pension scheme(s) unless these changes are already in place under the rules of those schemes.

Secondly, your employers have a number of options open to them under the new legislation. The most important of these are listed below under 'What your employers may do' in the form of a series of questions which you should put to your employer before you make any decision about your own future pension arrangements.

Compulsory changes

Your employers **have** to make these important changes to their present scheme, with effect from 6 April 1988 onwards, unless these requirements are already in operation:

(a) Membership of the pension scheme can no longer be compulsory, unless the scheme is non-contributory and provides death-only benefits.

(b) 'In-scheme' AVC arrangements have to be available (see Chapter 5).

(c)   Preserved benefits for members who leave the scheme after two years service have to be provided.

And, if your pension scheme is contracted-out, then in respect of any GMPs built up for service after April 1988:

(d)   Provide widowers' GMPs as well as widows'.

(e)   Provide annual cost of living increases (the lower of the Retail Price Index increase, or 3%) to future GMPs in payment.

What your employers may do

Your employers also have some other, equally important matters to consider in the next few months, including:

(a)   Will they allow membership of the pension scheme to become voluntary *before* April 1988, to allow you and others to opt out earlier if you wish to?

(b)   Will they continue to provide life assurance cover to employees who have opted out of or decline to join their pension scheme?

(c)   Will they allow you to rejoin their pension scheme later if you subsequently realise you made the wrong decision when you opted out? If they will, on what terms will you be able to return?

(d)   If their present pension scheme is contracted-in, will your employers take advantage of the 2% DHSS incentive payment by contracting-out from April 1988 up to 5 April 1993?

(e)   Will they decide to wind-up the present pension scheme altogether, to save future employer contributions?

(f)   Will they make any contribution towards your personal pension? (Most seem unlikely to).

(g)   What sort of 'in-scheme' AVC facilities do or will they allow?

(h)   If you decide to opt out of membership of the pension scheme but remain in your employers' service will they allow transfer of rights accrued under the pension scheme prior to April 1988?

(i) Based on their past record, are your employers likely to increase the benefits under their pension scheme from time to time over and above what the law requires? And will pensions paid under the scheme still be increased regularly each year by a minimum percentage or on some other basis?

(j) What changes do they intend to make to the present scheme to make it more attractive to you and other members? In particular, will they

- offer a money purchase scheme instead (possibly a contracted-out money purchase scheme, known as a 'COMP')?

- improve transfer benefit values, particularly to younger members and to those who leave after only a few years service?

- reduce your rate of contribution to the pension scheme, or even make it non-contributory?

- introduce, as an alternative to the pension scheme, a group personal pension plan under which your employers would negotiate a special arrangement for their employees with a particular personal pension plan provider?

It is essential that you should try to find out the answers to all these questions, before you make any decision about how you wish to provide for your pension in the future. More about this in Chapter 9.

7
Pensions from the State

This book would be incomplete without some further explanation of the pensions available through the State.

There are two principal pension rights:

(a)   The basic State flat-rate or 'old age' pension

(b)   A pension from the State Earnings-Related Pension Scheme ('SERPS')

plus various others such as older person's pensions, and pensions to war widows, to widows under industrial death benefits, and under the old graduated pension scheme.

The basic State flat-rate pension

This pension is available to everyone who has made enough national insurance contributions (or who is the widow of a contributor). It is not payable before men reach age 65, women age 60.

Current rates per week		6.4.87 – 10.4.88 £	From 11.4.88 £
Single person		39.50	41.15
Married couple – wife non-contributor:	joint	63.25	65.90
– both contributors:	each	39.50	41.15
	joint	79.00	82.30

The State Earnings-Related Pension Scheme (SERPS)

SERPS began in 1978, when the Social Security Pensions Act came into force.

All employees who do not belong to a contracted-out pension scheme have to participate in SERPS. However, as explained in earlier chapters, it will soon be possible for individuals to contract-out of SERPS through an appropriate personal pension plan, perhaps taken out instead of being a member of a pension scheme. Members of contracted-in schemes may also be able to contract-out through a 'free-standing' AVC which is approved by the OPB as being equivalent to an appropriate personal pension plan (see Chapter 5).

So far, only defined benefit pension schemes have been able to satisfy the OPB requirements on minimum benefits to enable them to contract-out. However, from April 1988, defined contribution pension schemes will also be able to contract-out if they meet the OPB's new alternative requirements on minimum contribution levels.

Pension benefits under SERPS

When introduced, and until last year, SERPS provided a pension equal to **one-eightieth** of revalued average* band earnings i.e. between the lower earnings limit and upper earnings limit, for each year in the scheme, **up to a maximum of 20 years** i.e. a maximum of $^{20}/_{80}$ths or one quarter of revalued average band earnings. If the employee had completed more than 20 years by retirement date, the pension was based on the average of the best 20 years' revalued band earnings, not necessarily the final 20 years'.

> * *Revalued average* band earnings means that earnings (i.e. pay) are revalued in line with the increase in national earnings each year, and so are virtually inflation-proofed.

The SERPS pension is only payable at State retirement age (65 for men, 60 for women) but may be deferred to 70 and 65 respectively.

Under the Social Security Act 1986, the government, expressing concern at the long-term costs of SERPS, reduced these benefits to all those **retiring** after March 2000. From then on, the pension will begin to be based on **lifetime** average earnings (not the best 20 years), and the maximum benefits will fall over a period of 10 years to one-fifth, not one-quarter, of revalued average earnings.

It will be obvious from the above that SERPS represents better value in return for contributions paid by employees due to reach State retirement age before the year 2000, (i.e. men now aged 52 or over and women now aged 47 or over), than for younger employees.

As contributions to SERPS are made via national insurance, they do not attract tax relief like contributions to pension schemes or personal pension plans. SERPS thus represents poorer value for those employees on the higher rate of income tax. Those higher paid employees may need to make other provision for their retirement to the extent that SERPS pension benefits are only based on their 'band earnings'.

You can find out your pension SERPS entitlement by completing the form contained in DHSS leaflet NP38 and posting it to Newcastle. (NP38 is obtainable from local DHSS offices.) Within a few weeks, the DHSS will provide you with an 'additional pension' statement showing: (a) the amount of your SERPS pension earned so far (or to previous 5 April) at today's values; (b) an estimate of what SERPS will provide as pension if you continue working to normal state pension age; and (c) an estimate of the SERPS pension at that date if your future earnings increase faster than prices. The statement will be accompanied by an explanatory leaflet (NP39).

8
Other matters to consider

Pension mortgages

A pension mortgage is a loan to enable the participant to purchase (or improve) a house. It differs from other types of mortgage because it is repayable out of the tax-free cash sum available from a pension scheme or personal pension plan on the borrower's retirement. Only interest is payable on the loan until it is repaid in full. The loan outstanding is also usually covered by life assurance or some other form of assignable life cover until normal retirement date.

A pension mortgage does not mean a loan given to you by a pension scheme or personal pension plan.

The advantages of a pensions mortgage are, briefly:

- Lower outgoings than under a conventional mortgage

- Tax efficiency and flexibility

- Favourable terms are usually available

The disadvantages are:

- Unless you make other savings arrangements during your working life, the lump sum remaining after you have repaid the pensions mortgage on retirement may reduce your post-retirement income (or capital) below the level you need.

- Complications can arise if you leave your present employment before retirement.

- Unforeseen circumstances such as early retirement or redundancy can also cause problems.

In recent years pension mortgages have become increasingly available through S.226 policies and AVC arrangements.

They will almost certainly be offered as a particular advantage of personal pension plans. However, a growing number of employers are now also beginning to make pension mortgage facilities available to members of their pension schemes. So if pensions mortgages interest you, find out what your employers' pension scheme may be offering in comparison with any personal pension plan you may be considering.

Gaps in normal employment

These can arise, for example, if you are away from your employment through:

- disability, e.g. a serious accident

- illness

- an overseas posting

- maternity leave

- enjoying a sabbatical or extended leave

(a) Pension schemes

The effect of the gap in your employment will depend on the trust deed and rules of your employer's pension scheme, but will usually mean

- In a final salary scheme, the loss of that period of qualifying service for calculating your pension benefit on the 1/60th or 1/80th formula.

- In a money purchase scheme, the loss of contributions during the period of absence, which means in turn less funds for the purchase of an annuity when you retire.

Your employer may be prepared to negotiate special arrangements with you. For assignments overseas, for example, they would be likely to continue to contribute to the pension scheme so that you do not suffer any loss of pensions benefit.

(b) Personal pension plans

You cannot contribute more than the maximum you are allowed in any tax year i.e. normally 17½% of your 'net relevant earnings' (see Chapter 4). So if your earnings are lower because of your absence, your contribution for that tax year may have to be less.

Early retirement

(a) Pension schemes

Retiring before the normal retirement age set under your employers' pension scheme's rules will obviously normally reduce your pension benefits because

- less contributions will have been paid into the scheme on your behalf by both employer and you

- the cost of purchasing an annuity will be higher.

However, if you are retiring early at the request of your employer, e.g. through redundancy, you should expect to be able to negotiate a pension in value somewhere between the minimum one to which you are entitled now and that which you would have expected to receive had you continued in employment until normal retirement date.

(b)   Personal pension plan

Again your pension will be less than expected at normal retirement date for the same reasons as set out in (a) above. As your employer will not normally be contributing to your personal pension plan, you have less hope of receiving any financial help from him to improve that pension.

Late retirement

(a)   Pension Schemes

You may wish, or be asked, to continue to be employed beyond your retirement age laid down in your pension scheme. Whether you or your employer will continue to make contributions to the scheme on your behalf will depend on the rules and trust deed of the scheme. In any event, though, your pension is likely to increase because of your late retirement to reflect the lower cost of an annuity as you get older and, in a money purchase scheme, the growth each year in the value of your part of the scheme from investment income and capital appreciation even though contributions in to it have ceased.

(b)   Personal pension plans

You can continue to contribute to these up to the age of 75.

Death in service

(a)   Pension schemes

Your employers' pension scheme is likely to provide protection for you and your dependants through

- **Life assurance cover** – a tax-free lump sum usually equal to a multiple of your gross annual pay (up to the Inland Revenue maximum allowed of 4 × gross annual pay)

- **A widow or widower's pension** – often equal to one half (or some other proportion of) the pension you would have received under the pension scheme's rules had you remained in your present employment at your rate of pay at the date of your death until your normal retirement age.

(b) Personal pension plans

Protection for your dependants is likely to be an additional cost under your personal pension plan, over and above the contributions made to secure your own pension.

For example one major life assurance company recently quoted the following rates for additional cover under its present personal pension plans (which are technically S.226 policies):

A   **Cost per £1,000 term life assurance cover (annual premium) for males†**

Insured's present age	Until age 60 £	Until age 65 £
20	1.45	1.57
25	1.50	1.67
30	1.81	2.08
35	2.46	2.89
40	3.53	4.20
45	5.14	6.12
50	7.41	8.80
55	7.90	12.36
60	–	12.27

† For females, the cost will be similar but at age advanced by 5 years i.e. cost p.a. at age 45 will be approximately £3.53 until age 60, £4.20 until age 65.

B   **Cost for male providing a pension of £100 p.a. to his widow assuming she is 3 years younger than him (annual premium)**

Insured's present age	Until age 60 £	Until age 65 £
30	3.22	3.85
35	4.14	5.00
40	5.33	6.61
45	6.89	8.57
50	8.74	10.99
55	10.36	13.67
60	–	15.56

The cost for a female providing a widower's pension will be substantially less than these figures.

Death after retirement

(a) Pension schemes

Many pension schemes now guarantee your pension for five years after it begins, so that if, for example, you die within one year of retirement, your 'estate' will receive a further four years' worth of pension, often in the form of a lump sum.

Most pension schemes will also pay your widow or widower a pension for the remainder of her or his life. Schemes vary on what they provide, but the amount normally relates to the pension you were receiving at the date of your death e.g. one half of that pension.

Increases in pensions made by your pension scheme after you retire would also usually be applied to widow's or widower's pensions.

These are very valuable benefits.

(b) Personal pension plans

The protection provided for your widow or widower will depend on the terms of the plan you negotiate and agree with the provider.

Commutation of your pension to provide extra widow's or widower's pension

Some pension schemes will allow you to elect, at the time of your retirement, to take less pension yourself for the rest of your life so that after your death your widow or widower (if she or he survives you) can receive a higher pension for the remainder of her or his life. The scheme's actuary will work out what the figures will be, to enable you to decide if you wish to choose this option. Personal pension plans will probably offer the same facility, as it does not cost the scheme or plan anything to implement.

Leaving service prior to retirement

(a) Pension schemes

Under a final salary (or defined benefit) scheme you can suffer a considerable loss in the value of your ultimate pension, particularly if you leave your present employer at a comparatively young age.

You incur this loss on leaving a final salary pension scheme because the benefits of leavers do not increase as rapidly as the benefits of stayers over the period up to retirement. If you stay with your pension scheme your pension will increase each year in line with your earnings. But if you leave your pension, at best, will increase in line with prices. For younger leavers the difference between increases in earnings and increases in prices can mean a big difference in the pension ultimately payable.

In practice many schemes do not even increase the benefits of leavers in line with prices, sticking instead to the minimum allowed i.e. no increases at all on benefits in respect of service prior to 1 January 1985 and increases in line with the lower of prices or 5 per cent each year for benefits for service after that date.

Since earnings are expected to go up faster than prices your benefit expectations are less when you leave a final salary scheme. This fall in value is often reflected in the transfer value which is payable. Some schemes, however, now provide what is known as a 'money purchase guarantee' which can increase the transfer value, particularly for younger members.

Under a money purchase scheme your transfer value will be the value of the contributions you and your employers have made during your service with them, plus interest from, and any capital growth in, the scheme's investments. This is likely to give you better value than a typical final salary scheme transfer calculation.

(b) Personal pension plan

The plan belongs entirely to you, and moves with you from job to job without any loss at all.

9
How to decide what to do

You now have to choose between the alternatives available to you in your category of employment as explained in Chapter 3.

This chapter contains some unbiased, independent advice and guidance to help you make that important decision.

Basic principles

Before considering the specific choices you can make, there are some basic principles worth remembering:

(1)   **The more you pay in, the more you get out**

That sounds obvious (and is). The point to be made, though, is that pension schemes, AVC schemes, and personal plans should all achieve broadly the same rate of investment return (interest, dividends and capital growth) as they all enjoy the same exemptions from tax on their income, and on capital gains made from the sale of their investments.

Therefore the more contributions that are made to a scheme or plan, the more benefits should emerge.

(2)   **For the majority it will be better to remain a member (or to join) your employers' pension scheme**

The main reasons are:

- Because your employer will be making contributions (often substantial) to the pension scheme for your and other members' benefit. It is expected that most employers will **not** wish to contribute towards personal pension plans.

- The pension scheme usually also provides valuable other benefits (life assurance, widows' or widowers' pensions etc.) which will cost you additional contributions under a personal pension plan (see Chapter 8).

- The pension scheme has the employers' backing. In final salary schemes, they undertake to make whatever contributions are necessary to provide the 'defined benefits' and often also give discretionary increases to pensions in payment.

- Expenses of pension schemes are usually borne fully by the employer. On personal pensions there will be deductions.

However there are some exceptions to this general rule, as explained on page 60.

(3)   Investment returns are very important

Pension scheme actuaries sometimes remind employers that, as a 'rule of thumb' an annual improvement of 1% (i.e. from say 7% to 8%) in the rate of return from investments (interest, dividends and capital growth) can mean a reduction of as much as 20% in the contributions required to meet benefits in final salary pension schemes. Alternatively – and preferably from your point of view as a member – the improved finances of the pension scheme can be used to increase scheme benefits.

In money purchase pension schemes or in a personal pension plan, the rates of investment return are equally important. The sum available at your retirement will increase if the rate of investment return rises. For example £1,000 p.a. paid in monthly instalments for 20 years will be worth £47,400 at 8% p.a. compound interest, and worth £53,200 at 9% p.a.

(4) In defined benefit schemes, younger members cost the scheme less than older members

The cost of financing a final salary pension scheme (where your pension will be based on your final salary and years of service) rises with your age.

Here is an example of a table of the contribution required at various ages in a pension scheme:

Age	Contribution as percentage of salary	
	Males %	Females %
20	8.8	8.4
30	10.7	11.0
40	13.3	14.5
50	15.9	17.1
60	19.1	–

(5) Your employers' reaction to the new legislation may be crucial

Remember to ask the questions in Chapter 6 *before* you make your pensions choice.

(6) Pensions are only part of your lifetime financial needs

Your decision on your future method of providing for your pension should not be taken in isolation.

Your decision may be affected, for example, by factors such as:

- your partner's (i.e. wife, husband or other) income and pensions expectations

- you and your partner's investments or other 'private' income

- the need to provide for heavy family expenses in the immediate future

- your and your partner's health

- how secure you feel in your present employment

- your life assurance policies or other pension expectations from previous employment.

Decisions to be taken

The choices now open to you were explained in Chapter 3. Your decisions can be reduced to four:

(1) **Should you rely on the State schemes only?**

(2) **If you are already a member of (or can join) a pension scheme, should you opt out in favour of a personal pension plan (or, prior to 1 July 1988 a S.226 policy)?**

(3) **Should you contract-out of SERPS (if you have that option)?**

(4) **Are AVCs worthwhile for you?**

(1) **Should you rely on the State schemes only?**

Almost certainly not. Chapter 7 indicates the pension you can expect from the State flat-rate scheme and from SERPS.

It is most unlikely that these two schemes alone will provide you with sufficient income to meet your needs in retirement.

Relying on the State schemes alone is not recommended for the great majority.

(2) **Pension scheme v personal pension plans (or S.226 policies)**

If you are already a member (or can join) a pension scheme should you opt out in favour of a personal pension plan? Four main reasons to favour a pension scheme in comparison with a personal pension plan were given earlier in this Chapter (see page 56). The table below sets out the particular circumstances or factors which you should also take into account:

	Favours a pension scheme	Favours a personal pension plan
Your age	Older	Younger
Expectation of leaving present employment	Low	High
Expectation about investment returns	Pessimistic	Optimistic
Expectation about your future pay increases	Faster than average	Lower than average
Level of employee contributions to pension scheme	Low	High
Past service rights in present pension scheme	Long service	Short service
Need to provide for dependants	High	Low
Extent to which you are prepared to take trouble to make own pension arrangements	Little extent	Great extent
Level of benefits in the pension scheme	Good	Poor
Entitled to the 2% incentive for a personal pension plan	No	Yes

Some people will have little difficulty in deciding. For example, if you are aged 45, in a good scheme, paying up to 5 per cent contributions, and expecting to remain in service up to retirement, there is little point in taking a personal pension. If you have any significant period of past service as well, the case is even more convincing.

On the other hand, if you are in your early twenties, optimistic about investment prospects and expecting to leave your employment in a year or so the personal pension is likely to offer the better choice. The only exception will be if the pension scheme provides that its benefits, even for early leavers, will be as good as those from a money purchase type scheme (or is indeed such a scheme). If you are in this position the pension scheme is likely to provide benefits equal to or better than a personal pension plan.

The chart which follows provides some further help if you are a member of **final pay scheme** which does not provide such a 'money purchase-type' underpin. It will help you choose whether or not you should take out a personal pension plan or belong to the employer's pension scheme **for the next year**. To get the optimum result you need to reassess this decision each year, since as you get older the answer will change.

Some people, because their employer requires them to make a once and for all choice cannot consider the matter year by year. Even in these circumstances, in practice you do have a chance to reassess your choice if and when you move to another employer with a pension scheme. However, if you are now in the position of having to make such a choice and you do not expect to change employment again you will certainly be better off in the pension scheme rather than investing in a personal pension plan.

In order to simplify matters it is not possible to consider every situation with every type of scheme, size of benefit and level of contribution. The cases covered by these charts are those which will apply to the great majority of pension scheme members. Look at the case which is nearest your own and then consider what difference the particular conditions of your scheme will make.

The sample pension scheme, for the purposes of this comparison with

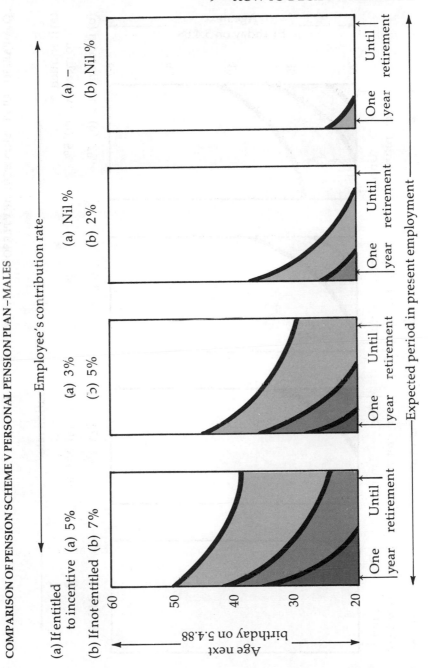

COMPARISON OF PENSION SCHEME V PERSONAL PENSION PLAN – MALES

— Employee's contribution rate →

(a) If entitled   (a) 5%   (a) 3%   (a) Nil %   (a) –
to incentive   (a) 5%   (c) 5%   (b) 2%   (b) Nil %
(b) If not entitled (b) 7%

Age next birthday on 5.4.88

60
50
40
30
20

One year — Until retirement

← Expected period in present employment →

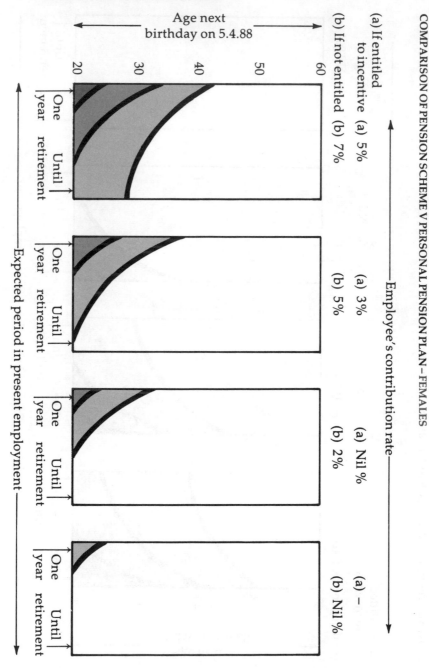

COMPARISON OF PENSION SCHEME V PERSONAL PENSION PLAN – FEMALES

Age next birthday on 5.4.88

Employee's contribution rate

Expected period in present employment

(a) If entitled to incentive (a) 5%
(b) If not entitled (b) 7%

(a) 3%
(b) 5%

(a) Nil %
(b) 2%

(a) –
(b) Nil %

One year retirement | Until retirement

a personal pension plan, is assumed to provide the following benefits, or some which when taken together are broadly comparable:

Pension: On retirement, at 65 for men and 60 for women, a pension equal to one sixtieth of earnings near retirement (*or* a pension of one eightieth plus a lump sum of three eightieths), for each year of service.

Pension increases: Pension benefits are expected to increase during payment but not fully at the rate of inflation.

Death in service: Either a lump sum of 3 or 4 times current pay *or* a lump sum of 1 or 1½ times pay plus a widow(er)'s pension.

Death in retirement: A widow(er)'s pension of about one half the member's pension.

Leavers' benefits: The statutory minimum or better.

The comparison therefore is for an average scheme. If your scheme is better than that assumed here (e.g. retirement is earlier or pension increases are higher) it will be that much better than a personal pension. Similarly if your scheme is worse, a personal pension will be that much more attractive.

To use the chart, follow these instructions:-

(a) choose the chart appropriate to your sex

(b) pick out the diagram with the contribution rate you are paying to your pension scheme. If you would be entitled to the 2 per cent incentive on a personal pension plan, take the figure along line (a). If you would not be entitled, take the figure along line (b).

(c) draw a line across the column at your age next birthday on 5 April 1988, **but** if you are already a member of the scheme add one year to that age for **each** year of past service for which you are entitled to benefits.

(d) draw a vertical line in your column depending on when you expect to leave this employment. Thus if you expect to leave after a year, the line will be on the left; if you expect to stay to retirement, it will be on the right; and if you expect to leave part way to retirement, the appropriate proportion across, e.g. if you are 35 and expect to leave after 15 more years service you would draw it half way across because 15 years is halfway to retirement.

(e) note in which part of the column the lines intersect. Depending on the shading of that area:

 It is certain that you will be better served by being a member of the pension scheme.

 If you are very optimistic about future investment returns and are not concerned about the other drawbacks of personal pensions, a personal pension plan is worth considering.

 A personal pension plan is worth considering, although there is still no guarantee that it will do better than your pension scheme.

In normal circumstances, it is likely that a personal pension is the better choice.

(3) Should you contract-out of SERPS?

Remember – you only have this way of contracting-out of SERPS if you are employed but not a member of a pension scheme. If you are a member of a contracted-in pension scheme, you may be able to contract-out of SERPS through a 'free-standing' AVC (see Chapter 5).

The main factors to consider in making this decision are set out in the following table, which shows the effect each of them has:

	Favours an appropriate personal pension plan*	Favours SERPS
Your age	Younger	Older
Expected investment returns	Optimistic	Pessimistic
Entitled to 2% incentive	Yes	No

* or equivalent free-standing AVC

Depending on your age, sex and whether or not you are entitled to the 2% rebate, you can trace on the chart on page 66 which of these choices is better for you over the next five years.

On the basis of your age at your birthday in the year following 5 April 1988 ascertain where you come in the column that applies to you.

Top Section: If you fall in the top section of your column you are almost certainly better off in SERPS.

Bottom Section: If you fall in the bottom section of your column you are likely to be better off with an appropriate personal pension plan – but remember this cannot be guaranteed.

Middle Sections: If you fall in the middle two shaded sections of your column more judgement has to be exercised about your choice. The main factor is whether you think investment returns on your personal pension plan will be high or low. If you fall in the upper part of this section then you have to be really optimistic to choose a personal pension plan. In this part returns would have to be significantly better than they have normally been in the past, for a personal pension plan to beat SERPS. Even in the lower part there is still a significant possibility that you might be worse off if you retire at a time when investments have performed badly. You may consider, at least in relation to this part of your retirement income, that you want a high degree of assurance about the pension you will receive. If so, you should remain contracted-in to SERPS.

IN OR OUT OF SERPS

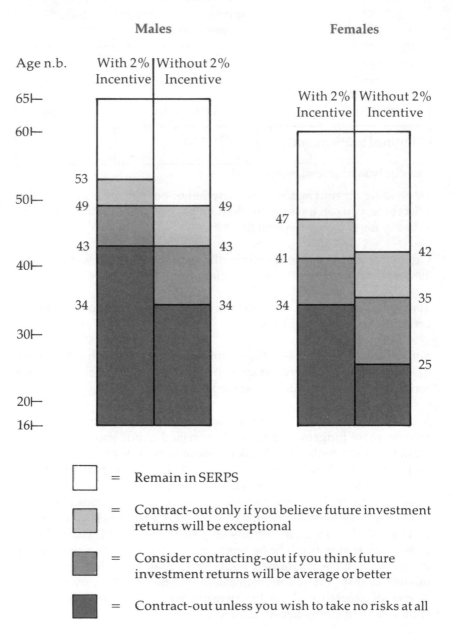

	=	Remain in SERPS
	=	Contract-out only if you believe future investment returns will be exceptional
	=	Consider contracting-out if you think future investment returns will be average or better
	=	Contract-out unless you wish to take no risks at all

After 5 April 1993 the terms for contracting-out will change and you should reassess your decision.

(4) Are AVC's worthwhile for you?

The normal advantages and disadvantages of AVCs and their other features, were explained in Chapter 5. You will recall that you can only make AVCs if you are a member of a pension scheme.

Examples of when you should make AVCs

- If you are aged 40 or over, and you know that your pension from your present and past pension schemes will be lower than the maximum permitted by the Inland Revenue.

- If you have surplus income after tax and want to improve your pension (subject to the previous point).

- If you are a member of a contracted-in pension scheme but wish to use a 'free-standing' AVC policy as a method of contracting-out of SERPS.

- If your earnings in any year are exceptionally high (perhaps from heavy overtime or from a profit-sharing bonus scheme), you can contribute up to 15% of those earnings, less whatever amount you have to contribute to your pension scheme, to an AVC policy.

Examples of when AVC contributions are not recommended

- If your pension from your pension scheme is already nearing the maximum allowed by the Inland Revenue.

- If you are young or youngish – say aged 35 or under – because money put in to AVC policies is untouchable until you reach retirement.

- If you are anxious to maximise your lump sum entitlement at retirement, as new AVCs can now only be used to improve pension benefits.

One final point on AVCs. You need no longer be concerned about whether you will be able to afford an AVC once started if you subsequently suffer a loss in pay, or some other financial crisis arises. This is because you can now vary the amount and timing of AVCs as you wish, subject to the overriding Inland Revenue limitations.

Conclusion

It will be clear from what you have read already that pensions in the UK have become an immensely complex subject. On the other hand, the government has created important new ways in which you can begin to provide for your retirement.

If after reading this short book you want further advice, you are recommended first to talk to the pensions expert at your employers or the firm of actuaries which is advising them on pensions matters. Local firms of accountants or solicitors may also now have someone who is knowledgeable about pensions matters.

If you do decide to take out a personal pension plan and wish to obtain independent advice on which plan to choose, you should consult an insurance broker (or any other adviser) who is authorised under the Financial Services Act 1986 through FIMBRA (the Financial Intermediaries, Managers and Brokers Regulatory Association).

You can also obtain advice from the following organisation about a suitable consultant:

Society of Pension Consultants
Ludgate House
Ludgate Circus
London EC4A 2AB
Telephone: 01-353 1688

Further copies of this book are available at leading bookshops throughout the UK or direct from the publishers (Tolley Publishing Company Ltd, 17 Scarbrook Road, Croydon CR0 1SQ). Please telephone them on 01-686 0115 if you would like a quotation for a bulk supply, or a special edition, for your firms' employees.

It is also supplied free of charge with a **20-minute video 'Pensions: Your Choice'** produced by Video Arts Ltd and with an **audio tape 'Your New Pensions Choice'**, presented by Louise Botting and produced by Tolley Publishing Company Ltd.

Appendix A

Effect of inflation

Both the purchasing power of the ultimate benefit and the real cost of contributions payable will depend on the rate of inflation over the period of the plan. By way of illustration the following table shows what £1,000 will be worth in today's money at the end of the periods shown if the annual rate of inflation over the period is as shown:

Period (years)	Purchasing Power of £1,000		
	3% Inflation	6% Inflation	9% Inflation
5	863	747	650
10	744	588	422
15	642	417	275
20	554	312	178
25	478	233	116
30	412	174	75
35	355	130	49
40	307	97	32

Source: The Rulebook of the Securities and Investment Board

Rights on leaving your Pension Scheme

When you leave your pension scheme you have the right to decide what happens to the benefits you have built up, **provided you have accrued benefits for at least two years (five years before 6 April 1988).**

These rights are yours under the law, from the Social Security Act 1973 including subsequent amendments. They apply whatever is actually said in the scheme rules, although the rights can be improved upon. If you have less than these periods of qualifying service there are no specific rights under the law. In contributory schemes it is normal, in these circumstances, to allow a refund of members' contributions but only if you are also leaving employment. It is also possible when leaving to get refunds from periods of service prior to April 1975 when earlier legislation came into force, although it is now unlikely to be worth your while to do so.

How you can use those rights

There are three options open to you under the legislation.

- a preserved pension;

- a transfer payment to a new scheme; or

- a transfer payment to an insurance company.

From 1 July 1988 it will be possible to make the transfer payment to any personal pension plan provider.

Preserved pension

You normally have the right to leave your pension in the scheme you are leaving. They (the scheme's trustees) have to preserve it and generally treat it on a par with the benefits of people who stay . Thus you must be given full credit for all past years of service. In final pay schemes the benefit will be based on your current pay but they are required each year to increase preserved benefits for service since 1 January 1985 in line with increases in retail prices (or 5 per cent, if less). From April 1988, the scheme will be able to transfer your benefits to an insurance company without your permission if you have less than five years accrued benefits.

Transfer to new pension scheme

Your old scheme is required to offer a transfer value, calculated on an approved basis, equal to the preserved benefits you have built up. It is up to your new scheme to decide whether or not it wishes to accept the transfer value – if it does it has to offer you benefits calculated on a basis compatible with the one it uses to calculate transfers out.

Transfer to an insurance company

As an alternative to taking your transfer value to your new scheme you can, instead, get it paid over to a life insurance company. This is sometimes known as a "Section 32 Buy-out" after the original legislation that facilitated this option. It is up to the insurance company whether or not it wishes to accept the payment and you will have to decide whether the terms they offer are acceptable. As mentioned above it will be possible, from 1 July 1988, to pay this transfer value to a personal pension plan as well.

Contracted-out rights

There are certain limitations on what choice you can make when leaving a contracted-out scheme. The scheme you are leaving is responsible for ensuring that your GMP rights are secure and this may lead, in certain circumstances, to your pension rights being dealt with in two parts.

Index

* = term defined in Glossary

INDEX

Glossary

Appropriate personal pension plan: one which satisfies certain conditions under the Social Security Act 1986 and is approved by the Occupational Pensions Board, which enables the contributor to the plan to be contracted-out of SERPS.

Approved pension scheme: one which meets certain requirements of the Inland Revenue, and which therefore enjoys the tax privileges outlined on page 6.

AVCs: additional voluntary contributions by a member of a pension scheme to increase his or her pension at retirement.

Band earnings: pay between the lower and upper earnings limits for national insurance (between £41 and £305 per week from 6 April 1988).

Contracted-in pension scheme: one whose members have not been contracted-out of SERPS.

Contracted-out pension scheme: one whose members have been contracted-out of SERPS, by being an approved scheme which satisfied certain conditions laid down by the Occupational Pension Board.

Contributory pension scheme: one to which both employer and members are required to make contributions, usually as a percentage of pay.

Defined benefit pension scheme: one under which the pension benefits at retirement are fixed (usually as ⅟₆₀th or ⅟₈₀th of final pensionable pay for each year of pensionable service), with the employer undertaking to make whatever contributions are necessary in addition to any members' contributions (which are usually a fixed percentage of pensionable pay). **Also known as 'final salary' scheme.**

Defined contribution scheme: one to which contributions by either or both employer and members are at agreed rates, the ultimate benefits being dependent on the size of the fund built-up, annuity rates at retirement dates, etc. **Also known as 'money purchase' scheme**.

Free-standing AVCs: additional voluntary contributions by a member of a pension scheme to an insurance policy or building society outside his or her pension scheme.

Guaranteed minimum pension (GMP): the minimum level of pension which a pension scheme has to provide in order for its members to be contracted-out of SERPS.

In-scheme AVCs: additional voluntary contributions by a member of a pension scheme to an insurance policy or building society chosen by his or her pension scheme, or to the scheme itself.

Leaving service: leaving an employer's employment, for any reason.

Net relevant earnings: earnings from employment or as a self-employed person, less deductions (other than personal allowances) which can be made to determine an individual's net income for tax purposes.

Non-contributory pension scheme: one to which only the employer makes contributions.

Pensionable salary (or pay): the pay on which a scheme member's pension will be based.

Pensionable service: employment which counts as years of service towards a member's benefit entitlement from a pension scheme.

Pension mortgages: a mortgage on which the principal (i.e. loan) is repaid out of lump sums which become available on retirement from pension arrangements of the borrower.

Pension scheme: in this book means any occupational pension scheme, i.e. one provided for employees by an employer, or a scheme open to employees within a certain trade or profession (e.g. the Social Workers' Pension Fund).

Personal pension/personal pension plan: new pension arrangement introduced under the Social Security Act 1986 and Finance Act (No 2) 1987. Enables an employee or self-employed person to make contributions to his or her own pension plan (see Chapter 4).

Revalued average band earnings: band earnings revalued in line with national earnings levels each year.

Section 226 policy/S.226 policy: one to which an employee not a member of a pension scheme or a self-employed person can contribute towards his or her own pension. On or after 1 July 1988, new S.226 policies have to be personal pension plans.

Section 32 buy-out: the option, on leaving a pension scheme, to transfer preserved benefits to an insurance company of your choice. Called after the legislation which first facilitated this choice.

SERPS: the State Earnings Related Pension Scheme which provides an additional pension based on pay in band earnings.

Notes

Notes

Notes

Notes

Notes

Notes

Notes

Notes